W9-BZM-230

THE STORY OF A SOUL

Theodore Marburg

THE STORY OF A SOUL

By
THEODORE MARBURG

Based, in outline, on Edith O'Shaughnessy's *"Life of Marie Adelaide, Grand Duchess of Luxemburg"* and on the Official Proceedings of the Luxemburg Parliament

PHILADELPHIA
DORRANCE AND COMPANY
Publishers

SECOND EDITION

MANUFACTURED IN THE UNITED STATES OF AMERICA

DRAMATIS PERSONÆ

WILLIAM IV, *Grand Duke of Luxemburg*

DUCHESS MARIE ANNE, *Consort of William*

PAUL EYSCHEN, *Prime Minister*

DUCHESS MARIE ADELAIDE DUCHESS CHARLOTTE DUCHESS HILDA DUCHESS ANTONIA DUCHESS ELIZABETH DUCHESS SOPHIE	*Daughters of William and Marie Anne*

COUNTESS ANNA MONTGELAS, *Lady-in-waiting to Marie Adelaide*

PRINCE XAVIER OF BOURBON-PARMA, *suitor for the hand of Marie Adelaide*

GUSTAVE, *huntsman*

HUSBAND WIFE CHILD	*Among the populace*

PRESIDENT, *Chamber of Deputies*

MINISTER OF STATE

HOFFMAN BECK HUSS PRUM THORN THELMAN JEAN SCHAACK PESCATORI BRASSEUR KREPS PROBST MARK SCHULTZ	*Members of the Chamber of Deputies*

PRELATES, COURTIERS, ATTENDANTS

THE STORY OF A SOUL

ACT I. SCENE I

Scene: Castle of Colmar-Berg. Enter: William IV, Grand Duke of Luxemburg, and Paul Eyschen, Prime Minister of Luxemburg.

THE GRAND DUKE:
The guns and churchbells, Eyschen! Hark!
That means
The child has come we have been waiting for.
The story of a soul is now begun.
Will it be tragedy or comedy?
Will that new soul be master of itself
Or will it be the slave of circumstance?
My wife and I can guard its babyhood,
Can set its early youth amid the rose;
But finally no safeguard will avail:
The soul itself must be the citadel.

EYSCHEN:
Aye, my liege! The loving care you give
To guard the health of body and of mind,
The precepts you instil to gauge life's values,

To guide the darling feet in awkward, dimly
Lighted ways, how little they avail
If there be lacking steadiness of purpose!
At the long last the soul must sail alone
And every man be helmsman of his own.

GRAND DUKE:

Nay, what is more, through no fault of his own
The best of captains yet may be o'erwhelmed.
This rock, whereon the Roman legions camped,
Against its base how often have misguided,
Blundering statesmen wrecked the peace of Europe!
Is this new soul to sail on calmer seas?
Or is it, powerless, to be engulfed
In some fresh wave of madness born of greed?
Yes, you are right, Paul Eyschen: guard our offspring
As we may, inform their minds by holding
Up to them the lamp of history,
There yet may enter, all unheralded,
That dark, mysterious element of fate
To crush relentlessly the stoutest soul.

There! The guns have ceased. You
counted them?
Ah, well! We must accept the disappointment
They proclaim. But, as you know, the Salic
Law does not apply to us and, if
No brother follow later on, this daughter,
Our first-born, may some day ornament
The throne of Luxemburg.
Come, Eyschen, I must
Hasten to the palace. Disappointment,
Keener than my own, 'tis certain, fills
The mother's breast and I must do my best
To lessen it.

Act I. Scene II

(*A lapse of fifteen years*)

Scene: Castle of Hohenburg, Lenggries, Bavarian Alps. Marie Adelaide sitting apart while her five younger sisters, hands clasped to form a ring, are frolicking and laughing as they dance.

CHARLOTTE:

Come, Marie. Do join us. Father calls you

Mouse; but that you're not. Mice love to play,
While there you sit, with gaze fixed on the ground
As if the earth were crystal and you could fathom
Happenings at the center.

MARIE ADELAIDE:

Let me be,
Sweet sister, let me be. I have my gloomy
Moods and cannot always throw them off.
At other times it is the pleasure which I
Find in my own thoughts that you mistake
For moodiness.

HILDA:

Come out into the sunshine.
See these jewels sparkling on the grass:
Such lovely diamonds, flashing green and blue
And yellow. Come dance with us and drink as deep
This morning air of our Bavarian Alps,
The softest, sweetest air in all the world.

ELIZABETH:

And see what fun we're having. Just watch Sophie.

She tripped and hurt her knee and now she's
hopping
On one leg and singing, silly thing,
"I feel like a morning star."
Oh! Look! There goes
A lovely humming-bird. You know, Marie,
That yesterday one poised itself and dipped
Into a flower so close to me, its fanning
Wings a mist, but all its iridescent
Body just as still as if there were
No motion of the wings. A moment so,
And then it flashed away to disappear
In a low tree hard by. I followed it
And climbed the tree and there I found its
nest
With oh! such darling, tiny eggs, pure white.
If you will come with me, I'll show it you.

MARIE ADELAIDE:

Not now, not now.

(*The dancing group settles down on the grass, singing softly and shaping wreaths of wild flowers. Charlotte leaves them and approaches Marie.*)

CHARLOTTE:

And may I sit beside you?

MARIE ADELAIDE:

Of course! I love to have you near. Your happy
Disposition, that lively interest
You take in people and in things, sweeps all
Before it. When you were born you bounced into
The world and looked around and straight exclaimed:
"My! My! How nice a place this is!"

CHARLOTTE (*Smiling*):

A most
Amusing way to put it; certainly
A pleasing one to me, though undeserved.
But, if my presence is a source of pleasure
To you, why still spend so much time apart
Even from me?

MARIE ADELAIDE:

I like to be alone.
One sees alone the things one cannot see
In company.
They wonder why I stay
Away so oft from family prayer and linger
So much at the church's door instead of

Entering in to share the common worship.
It is because I find myself made rebel
By the constant preaching of the fear
Of God and frightful future punishment.
To me, left in the open air, with all
The mystic beauty of the world about me,
There can be no such thing as fear of God.
For God is love. What men mistakenly
Call fear of God is fear of doing wrong.
The love of God is love of right, of keeping
His commandments. And God's forgiveness is
No other thing than the sweet healing nature
Brings to mind and body when we mend
Our ways.
Few churchmen will accept such a
Material view of great religious concepts.
None teach them: nor do books. And that is why
I like at times to be alone and take
My bearings for myself and of myself:
Direction's everything and distance nothing.
I know that I am young, that sorrow or
The sight of other's suffering may bring
A change and make of me, some day, religious
Devotee. But this I also know:

That I shall always linger honest to
Myself, whatever my convictions at
The time.

CHARLOTTE:

My darling sister, I am lost
In wonder, dear, whenever words so weighty
Fall from those sweet lips. As you have said,
It must be thinking, only thinking that
Matures the mind.

MARIE ADELAIDE:

No preaching, no! nor reading
Takes the place of it. And to think deeply
One must be alone, alone.

CHARLOTTE:

And yet,
You are too much alone. What's pleasanter
Or healthier than happy fellowship
With lively, kindred spirits?

MARIE ADELAIDE:

Nothing! I
Admit. And yet I like to be alone.

CHARLOTTE:

But surely, 'tis while shut up in your room
Or sitting thus alone that you get moody.
Whenever you consent to wander in
The fields or on the mountainside with us,
It melts away like wisps of cloud against
A breezy sky.

MARIE ADELAIDE:

Your simile has called
To mind some lines I wrote but yesterday,
That glorious, breezy yesterday. They show
How true your words are. Let me see. Why, yes!
I have them here.

(*Takes from her bag a sheet of paper and reads.*)

"With thrush that is flooding the grove with song,
With sweep of the elm as it sways;
With cedar of Lebanon clapping its hands
As in olden Bible days;
With flowing waves in the ripening grain
And ripples in the grass;
With purple peaks that climb to greet
The white clouds as they pass;

With sun and breeze and swaying trees,
All nature singing aloud;
With the sky's deep blue my heart sings, too,
And sails with the summer cloud."

CHARLOTTE:

Delightful! When you look and speak like that,
The Marie we so deeply love is come
Again.

MARIE ADELAIDE:

Of course I have my happy hours,
Yes! Many such.

CHARLOTTE:

Among the happiest,
I'm sure, are those of Christmas Eve when we
Six sisters fill our donkey cart with presents
For the poor and all start out together
To distribute them.

MARIE ADELAIDE:

Undoubtedly!
For, after all, is not enjoyment often
The reflected joy of those around us?
What more delightful than companionship

Of little children? And is it not because
The joy of children is so genuine,
So keen? To them the world is still all won-
der,
Their days so full of new discovery.
The young among all living things are gay:
The world belongs, my Lotta, to the young.

CHARLOTTE:

And you are young. Then why not share
the joy
That is youth's heritage?

MARIE ADELAIDE:

My moodiness
Is not without a cause. One by one,
In long procession, six of us, all girls,
Appeared upon the scene. Each time a son
Had been our parents' earnest hope.

CHARLOTTE:

But women
Have done well upon the thrones of Holland
And of Luxemburg, and two of England's
Proudest sovereigns have been queens.

MARIE ADELAIDE:

Quite true!

Quite true! And I am not unmindful of it.
But yet, as for myself, I often wonder
Whether I can worthily support
The heavy duties of a princely throne.
You've dreamed, I know, of some huge rolling thing
That's bearing down upon you in a narrow
Lane while you stand rooted to the spot,
Struggling in vain to move. Well! That is how,
By night, my future task appears. I see it
Otherwise by day: still fearsome, as a
Storm-cloud, dark, forbidding, but always fire-lined,
Superbly crimson, for I know that glorious
Moments are not stranger to a throne.

CHARLOTTE:

You have pictured vividly that most
Distressing, oft recurrent dream. But I,
Myself, more often dream the opposite.
I dream my palpitating hands support me
In the air while saying to myself
"This time I'm not asleep but proving to
My doubting friends that I can really fly."
Your lovely poetry, the bit you read
To me just now, is proof that you yourself

Can rise above the earth by day while I
Can only dream of it at night.

MARIE ADELAIDE:

And do you
Know just why that dream so often comes
To you? It is because, while lying on
Your bed, your feet are free: as little weight
Then rests on them as on a bird's in flight.

CHARLOTTE:

How nice
To have the curtain thus withdrawn from simple
Daily happenings we long have known
And have not fully understood. In some
Degree, perhaps, we all have intellectual
Curiosity which craves forever
To be satisfied.

SOPHIE:

You two are talking
Far too long. That odor of the pines
The sun is bringing out is making us
Impatient for our climb among them.

ELIZABETH:

Yes!
This meadow's beautiful; and yet I know,
Marie, you love, as much as we, the feel
Of that brown carpet of soft needles under
Foot, with moving sunlight flecking it,
Up there among the pines.

MARIE ADELAIDE (*Rising*):

Quite right! Quite right!
You've waited long enough. Just lead the
way
And you will find me quite as ready as
The rest to scale the steepest bit. We're off.
Why not to that high peak where one can see
All over this, our present world, and far
Into the next?

ANTONIA:

It's you, facetious lady,
That must lead us to that peak; we do
Not know it.

MARIE ADELAIDE:

Oh! yes, you do: Reflection is its
Name. But it can not be mastered in
An hour.

(The four who are seated on the ground leap up, spilling wreathes and flowers from their laps, and dash off the stage, Charlotte and Marie following more quietly. Curtain.)

Act II. Scene I

Scene: Castle of Colmar-Berg. Pink Room, Louis XV panelled. Marie Anne and Marie Adelaide, seated.

Marie Anne:

Alas! Your father, dear, is worse today,
Much worse. You know how long he has been ill?
Ten years! Ten years! Through all of them my every
Thought has been for him and all my pleasure
Tending him, to ease his suffering body
And console his troubled mind.
He was
So fond of life, made such rich use of it,
Was such a dear, dear husband. Before his health
Began to fail, how swiftly all the sunny
Hours glided by both here and in
High Hohenburg where two of you were born
And where we spent such happy, happy summers!

Of course he liked good company, good food,
And loved, above all else, the chase because
It took him in the open, to the mountains
And the woods. But if a lover of
The world, he was my lover, too, none more
Considerate.

MARIE ADELAIDE:

Mother, once he spoke
To me of lines he wrote to you but would not
Let me see.

MARIE ANNE:

Such tender lines! So sacred
That I keep them in that book that has
A clasp and key. While chamois hunting, just
Before he suffered his first stroke, he wrote
A lovely thing which often I take out
And hang upon. I would so love to have
You read it to me now.

(*Goes to desk, unlocks clasp of a small book and hands the poem to Marie Adelaide, who reads it aloud.*)

MARIE ADELAIDE:

"Last night I dreamed I was wooing
My gentle wife once more.

'Twas June and the perfume of roses
Stole in at the open door.
I doubted if roses as sweet as these
Had ever blossomed before.

Through fluttering casement curtain
Stray sunbeams played in her hair,
Delving deep in its shadows
And setting a glory there.
Had ever such gladdening rays from heaven
Illumined a head more fair?

Her rounded cheek and shoulder
A moment they caressed,
Then passed to the sprig of lilac
Close fastened at her breast.
The splendor they lent to the modest flower
No jewel ever possessed.

They set her delicate fingers
A moment all aglow
As the chasteness of alabaster
Is warmed by a light below.
Did ever the Renaissance painter portray
Fingers tapering so?

The swaying branch of the poplar,
Flashing its silver leaves,
Had set the sunbeams dancing
Along low-hanging eaves:
Chaste types of the gladness and purity
The maiden's presence breathes.

Over the emerald hillside,
Through oaks surmounting its crest,
We saw the clouds of summer
In billowy masses rest.
Such pearly hues the dreamer gives
To islands of the blest."

(*Dries her eyes*):

Mother dear,
You see the tears the touching lines have brought
To my own eyes and I can understand
All they must mean to you.

(*Goes over and pats her mother's shoulder.*)

MARIE ANNE:

Demonstrative
You never were, my child. A pressure of
The hand from you has ever meant as much
As close embrace of others. So when I see

Those rare, unwilling tears appear, I feel
That you are deeply moved indeed.

MARIE ADELAIDE:

I'm glad
You let me see the lines. They throw a light
On Father's mind and heart I was too young
To know.

MARIE ANNE:

The duties of a mother and
A wife, my dear, must ever be the richest
Life for woman and I look forward to
The time when you shall make a happy marriage.

MARIE ADELAIDE:

Ah! mother, that I fear will never be.
I cannot bear the thought of it. No! No!
I shall not marry.

MARIE ANNE:

What you have said would grieve me
Deeply, dear, did I not know that previous
Resolutions weigh but little when the
True mate appears. It is the heart, not reason,

That speaks then; and oft one finds the ways
Of love and reason merge.

(*A knock at the door: the doctor enters.*)

DOCTOR:

Pardon! Pardon!
I am but following instructions. I have
Come to bring the painful message that
The slender thread which holds his Royal Highness
Here may snap at any moment.

MARIE ANNE:

Go,
Marie, and summon all your sisters to
Their father's bedside. I will join you there.

(*Exit Marie Adelaide.*)

Ah me! Ah me! Although we know it to be
Blessed release from suffering, yet when
The dark, forbidding angel beckons those
Whom we hold dear and pushes wide the door,
That door through which we all must some day pass,
How trying the vast emptiness they leave!
I know beforehand I shall miss the very

Ministrations to him that absorbed
My waking hours and seemed a heavy burden
At the time.

ACT II. SCENE II

Scene: The Hall of Colmar-Berg. Marie Adelaide seen kneeling beside a bier. Enter Countess Anna Montgelas.

MARIE ADELAIDE:

How long have I been kneeling here?

MONTGELAS:

An hour
And more, dear lady; and I have ventured in
To break your lengthy vigil.

MARIE ADELAIDE:

You are so thoughtful
And attentive. Why is it you have ever
Been so good to me?

MONTGELAS:

The gentleness
And thoughtfulness that you display evoke
Like qualities in others, even as

A tuning-fork awakes and echoes lovely
Notes.

MARIE ADELAIDE:
That hour you say I have spent here
Has been a crowded one, an hour of tender
Memories, of new and deep convictions.
'Mong other things there passed in long procession
Through my mind my ancestors and those
Who ruled in Luxemburg before them.

MONTGELAS:
I know them
Well. How often we have delved together
In their histories!
Long, long ago,
So long that fact and legend blend in her
Came Ermesinde to found your hospitals
And schools.

MARIE ADELAIDE:
'Twas she who brought the charter of
Our liberties. They call her happy rule
Our "Golden Era."

MONTGELAS:

Early, too, there stepped
Upon the stage Elizabeth of Gerlitz,
Unforgetable because her nephew,
Sigismund, unwittingly made history
By selling, for a truly paltry sum,
The goodly Margravate of Brandenburg
To Frederick of Hohenzollern.
Among
Dramatic figures in the long procession
You have just reviewed must be, I know,
Your sightless hero, John of Luxemburg,
Who fell at Crecy. As I remember, 'twas
From out his helmet that the Black Prince plucked
The feathers three which he was wont to wear
And likewise took from him "Ich Dien," his motto.

MARIE ADELAIDE:

There came before me, next, that gifted child of
Charles the Bold, Marie Elizabeth.
Alas! her marriage tossed our Luxemburg
Into the Hapsburg's lap with, ah! such dire
Consequence to us, to Austria,

To France and to so much of Europe.
Throughout
How many generations Europe suffered
From the fateful rivalry created
By that marriage!

MONTGELAS:

Nor did you overlook,
I know, Don John of Austria, the natural
Son of that great sovereign of half
Of Europe, Charles the Fifth. With what
absorbing
Interest we followed all the lively
Story of his stirring deeds — that handsome
Conqueror of Moor and Turk and many
A woman's heart, but, in the end, no match
For stubborn and sagacious William, Prince
Of Orange.

MARIE ADELAIDE:

Of course Don John was there. One could
not
Overlook the hero of Lepanto.
They passed before me so impressively,
All these and many, many more, among them
Mother's forbears, the Braganzas.

MONTGELAS:

That house
Which gave to Portugal its line of kings
And to Brazil two emperors; that blood
To which you owe your own surpassing beauty
And their Highnesses, your sisters, their
Unquestioned loveliness.

MARIE ADELAIDE:

A blood that loved
And hated well, though I myself appear
Incapable of either passion.

This,
My Anna, was a dreaded moment: my dear
Father's death that places in my hands
The reins of government. Strange! now that
It is here, all sense of weakness and
Unworthiness is gone.

Aware of how
The velvet curtain of the night blots out
The lovely countryside, are we as conscious
Of that curtain of the day, the diffused
Light that steals from us the infinite?
For does not day blot out that starry space
The soul drinks in with awe when day is done?
Just so I find the crowded hours of

Informing day shut out perception of far
Deeper things. This lonely vigil at
My Father's bier has brought new understand-
ing:
Realization of the transience
Of worldly state and pomp, borne in on me
By my poor Father's suffering and death.
And, Anna, it has wrought a change in me,
A deep religious change and calm of soul;
Reliance on myself that was not there
Before. Ah! now I know the task before me
To be God-ordained. He, He will help me
Bear it.

(*Enter throng of people: members of the family and of the Court, prelates and neighboring sovereigns. Singing by the Choir, during which the bier is carried out. Curtain.*)

ACT III. SCENE I

Scene: Street in Luxemburg. Sidewalk lined with people facing roadway.

HUSBAND:

I hear the people shouting, do I not?

WIFE:

Yes, yes, but still far off.

HUSBAND:

She must be coming.
Eighteenth day of June! Why, this is then
The anniversary of Waterloo.

WIFE:

And our Grand Duchess was eighteen just four
Short days ago.

HUSBAND:

Springtime of life, my dear!

WIFE:

And she so lovely who is wandering through it!

I often meet her visiting the poor.
Those glorious, great blue eyes of hers! One
gazes
Long and deep in them and turns away
Reluctantly as from the restful depths
Of the blue sky. That shining hair that falls
So beautifully o'er that slender neck,
As graceful as was that of luckless Marie
Antoinette! And, then, the smallness of her
Foot surprises one. They say she's worn
The same-sized shoe since her eleventh year.
The shouts are nearer. John, pick up the child
Or he'll be crushed. Everyone is hungry
For a look at her and certainly
No passing glimpse will satisfy that throng.
They'll stream along the sidewalk in a vain
Attempt to keep the royal maid in sight.
Ah! There she comes.

HUSBAND:

And there's the surging crowd
Fast bearing down on us.

(*Cries of "Vive la Grande Duchesse," growing louder.*)

CHILD:

Look! Daddy, look!

Four horses to a shining coach. It's blue
And all the inside's shining.

MOTHER:
Lined with silk.

CHILD (*claps its hands in delight*):
And look! the horses! Everyone is prancing
Just as we do when we're playing horse.
How funny! There's no coachman on the box,
But two men riding on the horses' backs.
And oh! Just see that lovely lady there
Inside. It's like the fairy books. And real!

WIFE:
She hears you and is smiling at us. Hush!

HUSBAND:
And what a charming, charming, smile it is!
She must be conscious of her pearly teeth.
What bloom of youth and radiating freshness!
She plainly wears another crown besides
The crown of state: it's that of innocence.
No wonder that the crowd are mad about her.

WIFE:
And yet you know, John, some there are who would
Deny the throne to her.

HUSBAND:

Oh yes! In every
Country there are always men who seek
To change the form of government. With some
It is a matter of conviction. Others
Are sensationalists who wade against
The current with no other motive than
To make a ripple. Here in Luxemburg
The revolutionists have but little weight.
We are too small for a republic. What's more,
Our very dangerous position makes
A monarchy the better form for us.

ACT III. SCENE II

Scene: Chamber of Deputies. Marie Adelaide, accompanied by officials and suite, enters the Chamber and ascends the throne amid prolonged applause. The deputies are in their seats, diplomatic and public galleries filled.

MARIE ADELAIDE:

Although profoundly moved at being here
Among you, gentlemen, misgivings have I
None. My country's representatives
Have ever shown affection and respect

To my progenitors: to my long suffering
Father as to his, the Grand Duke Adolphe.
And lately, when my father passed away
Deep sympathy for my devoted Mother
Marked your speeches here.
Is not the child
Then justified in her assurance that
She, too, will have your loyal, full support?
My father's years of illness robbed me of
The chance to have, through him, a proper schooling
In diplomacy and government.
In this I am indeed unfortunate.
Yet, aided by your councils in discharge
Of all the serious duties resting on me,
I shall, perhaps, prove not unworthy of
The trust. The present duty is to meet
Requirement of the Fundamental Act
Respecting oath of office. This I do.
I swear the Constitution to observe,
Our independence and integrity
Of territory stoutly to maintain,
To guard the liberty and rights of all
By every legal means.
This I swear
To do. So help me God.

It would be rash
Of me to try, today, to sketch a program
For my reign. To tell you of my cherished
Hopes and aims alone is possible.
Permit me to confine myself to that.
Devoutly do I wish to earn the title
Of a good and worthy sovereign
Prescribed by that broad oath I just now took.
To help to realize in every way
The Beautiful, the True, the Good—is not that
A sufficient joy for any crown?
You know
How, on the Ducal Palace, there appears
The bas-relief of John the Blind, with his
Device, "Ich Dien," and on the self-same wall
The features of the Emperor, Henry Seventh,
Whose favorite motto was "Judge Justly."
The purpose
To conform to the demands of these two
Mottoes will inspire my every act.
The common good and law will be my guide.
Equal justice! Yes! But likewise justice
That protects the humble and the weak.
To give to men, in ever growing measure,
Equal opportunity must be
The grave preoccupation of our age;

For social peace, so ardently desired,
Thus far remains a high, unrealized
Ideal. To reconcile and to unite
Conflicting elements within the State—
What task more urgent or of vaster import?
If we appeal to that proud sense of justice
Deeply rooted in the human heart,
May we not hope that those eternal laws,
Which make for justice, will not fail, here too,
To operate, with gradual betterment
And finally with triumph to the cause?
To govern for the people, with the people
Was my father's constant aim. Only
With the people, he was wont to say,
Will we be able properly to solve
The serious problems which the future holds.
This, then, is my inheritance. Your own
Enlightened patriotism, gentlemen,
Will help me carry it with honor. May heaven
Bless our work.

We owe a lasting debt
Of gratitude to many heads of States
And many foreign Governments who showed,
In lively manner, their deep interest in

Our country and our Sovereign House. We shall not
Fail to cherish it in grateful memory.
The source of our prosperity must ever
Be the treaties international
That guarantee our independence and
Neutrality. Our rights are thus imbedded
In the law. But rights and duties are
Twin brothers. The treaties likewise place upon us
Obligations to the rest of Europe.
These we must respect. We must so act
That the correctness of our attitude
Can ne'er be brought in question.
Yes, I love
My country. Happy, proud am I to bear
Its name, to wear its crown. I seek no greater
Pleasure than to serve it and no greater
Privilege than to further, with your aid,
Its true prosperity and interests.
To the
Frail hands of a young girl the flag has this day
Been entrusted. She will hold it high
And firm and, by God's help, will fight to guard
Its honor.

Daughter of Nassau, I shall be faithful,
Like my ancestors, to the device
Born by our ancient house, "Je Maintiendrai."

THE PRESIDENT:
The nation's representatives are glad
To celebrate, within this hall, the advent
To the throne of their young sovereign,
Our first Grand Duchess born on our own soil.
Your Royal Highness has, from infancy,
Been cherished in our hearts, inseparable
From love of country.
At the center of
A Europe armed, the Duchy flourishes
As an oasis of God-given peace.
This very work of peace, of justice, social
Solidarity, as well as culture,
Art and charity—this Her Royal
Highness has declared to be the fair
Ideal of her smiling youth.
By leading
Some along the path of duty, while,
In other breasts, awakening confidence
And hope, our youthful sovereign's sure to make
Herself still dearer to us and to bind

More firmly still the bonds which now unite
Our people.

ACT III. SCENE III

Scene: Chamber of Deputies, seven years later. Groups standing conversing. The Chamber not yet in session.

HOFFMAN:

You are early, Bech.

BECH:

Yes! Yes! Such big
Events are in the offing I knew I'd find
A number of my colleagues here.
This question
Of our Sovereign's abdication possesses
All my thoughts and I would learn what turn
The matter takes. Her friends here in the Chamber
And among the populace at large
Are numerous enough. But can we save her
In the face of France's opposition?
(*Huss and Prum join them.*)

HOFFMAN:

I do not know. I find the situation
Cruel and unnecessary. To have
Dined the Kaiser, and allowed the royal
Family to appear so often in
The company of German officers,
Of course, was not discreet; but never was there
Actual breach of our neutrality.
Abet or aid the Germans we did not.
We had no army. Half a century
Ago, by order of the Powers, our proud
Old citadel was blown to bits.

So no one
Looked to us to war on an invader.
By that same token, Luxemburg, disarmed,
Has little power now to stem the tide
On either side in any future war;
She cannot help nor hinder friend nor foe.
Why, then, demand removal of our Sovereign?
A step so drastic is not justified
By her mere acts of courtesy to Germans
Nor by her German sympathies, if such
Exist.

PRUM:

Quite right! Quite right!

BECH:

'Tis less than seven
Years ago we placed, with so much pride,
That lovely girlish figure on the throne.
You remember she was gowned in white,
Her pearls and diadem enhancing the
Distinction of her tall and slender person.
And she has borne herself so well, with so much
Understanding and with dignity.

HUSS:

Aye! Aye! No breath of scandal e'er attached
Itself to Marie Adelaide nor to the
Other princesses. And what a handsome
Lot they are! It does one good to see them
All astride their lively, blooded horses,
Starting for a gallop in the woods.
And what a brave array they make at court!
We'd miss our dynasty were we to lose them.

PRUM:

What one admires in our Grand Duchess, too,
Is her consent to hear most patiently
Another's views while doing her own thinking.

When she and Eyschen clashed about religious
Teaching in the schools, there was no thought
In her of giving way. You must recall
The earnestness of her reply to him:
"But think upon the history of my people.
Their prayers have often been their only
bread;
And am I now to offer them a stone?"
There was a touch of eloquence in that.

HUSS:

And on that question she was adamant.
His resignation must have taken place
Had not that sudden heart attack removed
Poor Eyschen from the stage on which he long
Had been so great a figure.

HOFFMAN:

He had served
Four Sovereigns and had served them well.
That God-like
Head, we all so much admired, was not
Mere ornament.

BECH:

They say he had prepared
His resignation, even signed it, and that

The very controversy with the Sovereign
He so greatly loved was too much for
His strength. We know the Duchess, on her part,
Held Eyschen equally in high esteem.
She knelt in prayer beside his silent form
As she had knelt beside her father's bier,
And, when she rose, said simply: "How much wisdom
And what goodness will be buried in
That grave." She has a heart, our Duchess.

HOFFMAN:

Her goodness
And her charm are widely recognized.
The Belgian, Dutch and German Courts all fell
In love with her; and of her visit to
The Belgian rulers she herself exclaimed,
Appreciative soul, "Es war doch schoen."
So exquisite, so young! In such high station!
Was she not bound to make appeal to every
Heart?

BECH:

The session is about to open.

(*All members seek their places.*)

MINISTER OF STATE:

Peace has come, deliverance from the anguish
Of that foreign occupation which weighed
With heavy hand on all of us. Retreating
Troops, together with repatriated
Prisoners of war, those luckless souls
Who'd thought themselves abandoned of their God
But in whose breasts new hope had dawned—all these
Have passed across our land without mishap
And soon our public services should function
Normally again. Meantime I beg
Our people to be calm. We need not take
Too seriously the mobs and agitators
Seeking to o'erthrow our present form
Of government and set up a republic.
Extreme demands defeat themselves. One group
Of radicals would have the government
Consist exclusively of farmers and
Of laborers, allow the soldiers and
Police themselves to choose their officers
And have the State seize railroads, banks and foundries.

THELMAN:

Aye, and what is more, we'll not stop there.
You'll find us taking everything.
(*Laughter.*)

JEAN SCHAACK:

The measure's
Overdue. By that door long ago
The masses should have come into their own.

MINISTER OF STATE:

Another group demands the abdication
Of the House of Nassau.

PESCATORE:

Dynasties
Across the Rhine have abdicated; why not
Ours?
(*Protests from right.*)

BRASSEUR:

Exactly what our Liberal Party
Now demands: abdication which is
Voluntary. It must be voluntary
Since the Constitution guards our ruler's
Rights.

Religious ardor has subjected
Our Grand Duchess far too much to priestly
Dominance and secret influence.
When I
Questioned the then Minister of State
About the visit of Count Hertling, German
Chancellor, to Colmar-Berg, he said

He had not been consulted. Questioned then
On the betrothal of our sovereign's sister,
Young Antonia, to Rupprecht of
Bavaria, he made the same reply.
This proves the Ministry were not consulted
In acts of high importance to the state.

KREPS:

And for that very reason monarchy
Itself must ever be condemned: it lacks
Responsibility.

JEAN SCHAACK:

Quite right! The doctrine
Of God-given rule is nothing other
Than to say "Whom God gives public office,
To him is understanding also given."

PROBST:

The Crown should abdicate.

(*Cries of traitor.*)

BRASSEUR:

Through Monsieur Pichon,
Foreign Minister, the French declared
They would have naught to do with us so long
As Marie Adelaide was on the Throne,
And he refused to see officially
The delegation we had sent to Paris.

MINISTER OF STATE:

No accusation has been leveled at
The Sovereign of Luxemburg by any
Foreign Government whatsoever. The foreign
Press has done it, but we cannot act
On press reports.

PROBST:

Oh! Oh!

(*Laughter and noisy interruption.*)

THE PRESIDENT:

Gentlemen,
You may not interrupt.

MINISTER OF STATE:

Your mockery
Proves nothing.

MARK:

The facts are plain; you shut your eyes
To them.

BRASSEUR:

Do you believe the maelstrom of
Democracy that's sweeping o'er the world
And overturning thrones on every hand
Will stop at our door?

MARK:

At this moment
There is waiting in the street below
A delegation from a public meeting
Which voted to demand the abdication
Of our ruler. I ask that you receive them.

PRUM:

No! 'Tis a proceeding quite unheard of.

(*Interruptions. Confused noise.*)

THE PRESIDENT:

Unless the gallery abstain forthwith
From demonstrations, I shall be forced to close it.

(*Cries of "Oho! Oho!" Violent disorder in gallery.*)

THE PRESIDENT:

Empty the gallery!

(*Violent protests by the left.*)

BRASSEUR:

Afraid of the people!

(*Prolonged disorder.*)

THE PRESIDENT:

Conditions
Are impossible. The session is
Suspended.

Act IV. Scene I

Scene: Park of Colmar-Berg. Marie Adelaide and Prince Xavier of Bourbon-Parma are seen strolling about.

Xavier:

I've come to woo you, cousin. You were always
Dear to me and when my sister, Zita,
Married Charles of Hapsburg and I caught
That glimpse of you in budding womanhood,
So shy, so lovely—you were then sixteen—
A pure white blossom in the happy throng,
I felt at once 'twas more than boyhood fancy
That had mastered me. Had inclination
Triumphed then, you know what I had done?
Neglected all my home affairs to follow
You to Luxemburg and there lay siege
To that proud heart of yours.

Marie Adelaide (*Smiling*):

Oh, my! 'twas well
That duty and not impulse triumphed there.

I hear you've managed admirably your father's
Fair estate of Pianor' de Lucca,
While siege of this unfeeling heart of mine
Had been so profitless.

XAVIER:

Your heart is not
Unfeeling, else report of all your doings
Must be false. And that sweet face, so thoughtful,
Tender and so honest, likewise tells
A different tale.

I see you from afar
As beautiful as some lone watcher on
The hillside finds the far cathedral pile
The sun is lingering on caressingly
While all the land about it is in shadow.
And when, from time to time, my lonely path
Meets yours, I find myself the more subdued
To your rare qualities until my own
Identity seems merged in yours and I
But live and breathe in you.

I'm hungry for
Your love, Marie. If only, for all time,
I could be near you! Tell me so and you will
Open wide the gates of heaven to me.

MARIE ADELAIDE:

Oh! see that darling ripple in the brook
The sun has just picked out and that resplendent,
Deep green moss o'erhanging it!

XAVIER:

Aye, cousin,
Colorful and glorious as that spot
My future years if you would share them!
Your presence
Brings me infinite content. It is
As restful as the woods or twilight hour.
With you beside me, all the field of man's
Endeavor broadens, deepens, life itself
Means more.
When a boy, I found the days
And weeks so rapturously long. The joy
Of wading in the brook on matted willow
Roots; of running down young rabbits to take
Home; of capturing a fluffy fledgling
To imprison in one's hand awhile;
And of that shameful practice, robbing birds' nests!
One day I reached into a nest above
My head and found a snake coiled there. The nests

I robbed were fewer after that.
What endless
Sunny hours I spent in swaying treetops,
Singing, shouting till the hillsides answered
Back; in parting the tall grass or lying
Down in it to follow with the eye
A soaring hawk or watch the antics of
My kite as the breeze freshened with a passing
Cloud and that delicious pull upon
The string grew stronger!
Now the pressure of
Affairs at home makes weeks and months
A whirling wheel in which the spokes—the
days—
Are indistinguishable.
Quite otherwise
I find it here 'neath interlacing beeches,
Letting sunlight through to play upon
That lovely head of yours.
In carefree, idle
Wandering with you—you lay upon
My soul a hand so quieting—one has
A chance to question "Whereabouts" and
"Whither."
Borne in on me today, as ne'er before,
The deep conviction that the "Whither" of

My life depends on you! And just because
Your happiness, Marie, is dearer to me
Than my own—although, God knows, I long
For you—I feel impelled to add: the
"Whither"
Of your life, mayhap, depends on me.
The attitude assumed by France toward
Your person points the need of taking, as your
Mate, someone, like me, who wore the Allies'
Uniform throughout the war.

MARIE ADELAIDE:

Look there!
That doe came down the wind and has not
scented
Us. And see her pair of dappled fawns
Just breaking through the brush! How sweet
they are!
She stops. We're seen. And look! how fear-
lessly
She holds her ground until the frightened
fawns
Have scampered off! Now she herself makes
off.
And with what grace!

Last year I had a like

Experience. You know that shady glen
Of hemlocks where this crystal stream drops
down
O'er mossy rocks. One morning I was idling
On my horse down there, the reins left dan-
gling
On his glossy neck while I was lost in
Thought, when, in the road ahead of me
And moving straight at me with trailing
wings,
There came a mother partridge. "Certainly,
Good madam," I exclaimed, and stayed my
horse
Till mistress partridge gathered up her chicks
And led them off the road.

XAVIER:

I am not blind
To the bewitching and the naive way
In which you seek to change the channel of my
Thoughts and stay my pleading. But I'm as
fondly,
Foolishly and hopelessly in love
With you as anyone whose tale was ever
Told in song or story. I could repeat it
Every hour of the day and then not

Tell it you as often as I would.
To everything that's beautiful and noble
You belong and naught appears complete
Without you. Dear to me this land of roses,
Luxemburg, because it is the land
Where you were born and grew to womanhood
In gardens which have come to be a part
Of you. Another part reflects the virtues
Of your summer home in the Bavarian
Alps. Your gentleness was born of its
Soft winds, the rhythm of your step of swaying
Branch, and in your eyes are dancing sunbeams
Caught up in its woods.

MARIE ADELAIDE:

Gardens fade.
The rose's petals fall. So, too, the lovely
World I've lived in soon will be no more
For me. Fate has decreed it otherwise.

XAVIER:

But you are still quite free to choose. Now and
Then inexorable fate, as Greek
Tragedians often pictured it, o'ertakes
The innocent. But far more often 'tis

The blinded mind that is to blame. I beg
Of you, Marie, to make no wrong decision
Now. Accept my love. The very hills and
Streams all know I love you; they are ever
Whispering your name to me. And loving
You so much, am I not sure to make you
Love me too? The truest love, they say,
Comes after marriage. Couples who have lived
A long and happy life together, sharing
Joys and sorrows, having common thoughts,
In some strange way may even come to look
Alike. The soul, of which the countenance
Is but an index, tunes itself to that
Sweet marriage vow.
Then come to me and let me
Wrap the warm cloak of my love about you,
Shielding you.

MARIE ADELAIDE:

I cannot give my answer
At this moment, Xavier. The sorrow
Of the world, its deeds of violence,
Its shame were spread so constantly before me
By events and Acts of Parliament
I had to sign, that I have long outgrown

My early unconcern about religion.
I have come to look on it as the
Great need of man.
                    What utter disregard
Of all God's laws I've witnessed, laws men feebly
Place on statute books but the true home
Of which is in the human heart!
                    In that
Dread war we witnessed millions swept away
In their young manhood. Nursing them I often
Saw their souls rebellious at approaching
Death. How can one turn to thought of one's
Own welfare after months of that?
                    Example
Carries further than the spoken word.
I cannot preach, but I can spend a life of
Self-denial within silent convent
Walls, ignoring all its physical
Discomforts and concerned alone with matters
Of the soul.

XAVIER:

                    But you have been so useful
In the world. This tragic aftermath

Of the World War demands especially
Such helpful presences as yours. Could there be
Richer offering to God than your
Devotion to your people's good? Then why
Become a part of that brown carpet of
Dead leaves that convents are?

MARIE ADELAIDE:

Dead leaves make up
The wood-mould that sustains the forest life.
So matters of the soul enrich our lives.
And meditation within cloistered walls,
Disclosing some new truth about the soul,
Is fully justified.

(*Enter five sisters on horseback.*)

ANTONIA:

Oh! there you are!
We've searched the forest for you. The forester
Has seen so many shrubs uprooted. Wild boars,
With tusks of fearsome size, he says, have wandered
In from the Ardenne. He warns us not

To venture out afoot till he has rid
The woods of them.

ELIZABETH:

Besides its nearly time
For lunch and that most joyous exercise
Cannot take place till you and Xavier
Are there. Come, jump up on our horses with us.
Unless the brutes decide to rid themselves
Of an unwelcome load and spill us without
Warning on the way, we'll have you both
At home forthwith.

MARIE ADELAIDE (*smiling*):

Madcap! The suggestion's
Worthy of you.

CHARLOTTE:

Then, we will be your mounted
Bodyguard; two riders in advance and
Three to guard the rear. Why, yes! 'Twill be like
Carrying back two prisoners of war
And make a brave parade of Amazons.

MARIE ADELAIDE:

Be off with you. We'll follow leisurely.

Enamoured of each other's company,
We do not mean to hurry. And, oh! be sure
To trample down some full half-dozen of
Those fearsome boars and bring their gory heads
To me.

THE SISTERS (in chorus, laughing.)
We will!

(*The restive horses are given rein and are off at a gallop.*)

XAVIER:

How can you think of leaving
Such a galaxy of lively girls?
A life spent in seclusion! No! No! No!
'Twould throw you back too much on your own thoughts.
Sunshine and the rose belong together.
You are too glorious a flower to be
Lost to us.

MARIE ADELAIDE:

I like you, Xaxier:
You are a thoughtful man. That I like,
And I like, too, the bit of mysticism
In your nature; for you the unknown, too,

Exists and must be reckoned with. Tonight
You'll have my answer to your question.
Gracious
Me! what's this?

(*Crashing of bushes, followed by the charge of a wild boar. Xavier abruptly pulls Marie Adelaide toward him and the boar's tusks rip her skirt.*)

XAVIER:
He's sure to turn. Quick! Jump
Behind that tree.

(*The boar turns and makes for Xavier who leaps aside and eludes him. Before the creature can turn again a shot rings out and it falls to its knees. The forester appears and smashes its head with the butt of his rifle.*)

MARIE ADELAIDE:
'Twas timely, Gustave. We are
Deeply in your debt.

GUSTAVE:
I feared your Highness
Was not safe, so have been seeking you.
Wild boars are ugly fellows and their ire
Is kindled by mere sight of us.

MARIE ADELAIDE:

Thank you,
Gustave, thank you many times.

(*Goes up and extends her hand to him.*)
(*Curtain*)

ACT IV. SCENE II

Evening of the same day.

Scene: Salon in Palace, city of Luxemburg. Charlotte, Elizabeth, Antonia, Hilda, Sophie, Xavier, Montgelas and members of the Court Circle are seen standing or moving about in groups. Marie Anne and Marie Adelaide are seated close by, now conversing, now glancing in amusement at the nearest group on overhearing their remarks.

XAVIER:

How well you look tonight.

HILDA:

It must be dark
In here.

XAVIER:

And what a most becoming gown!

HILDA:

It must be growing darker.

SOPHIE:

'Tis the gown
She wore a fortnight hence and carried all
Before her at a jolly dance we all
Attended.

HILDA:

I had a wondrous time that night
Despite the tiny man, Prince Miniscule,
Who claimed so many dances of me. You know
We sisters, Xavier, are fairly tall;
At times I thought I'd lost him on the floor.

SOPHIE:

Yes, yes! I now recall him peeping out
From underneath your arm. I wondered, later
On, about the powder patch atop
His head.

HILDA:

But oh! I did have a good time!
Such lively neighbors at my table at
The supper! And, sister, what an imbecile

I was, the following week, to call our host
Of that delightful dance by the wrong name.
Would you believe it, Cousin Xavier,
I actually mistook him for a man
Whose guests we were the following day,
A man he heartily dislikes.

XAVIER:

Oh, well!
You got him on your meal list anyway.
And, Hilda, I am sure your memory
Does not often play you tricks. They tell me
You were honored by an invitation
To address a woman's club the other
Day. What did you talk to them about?

HILDA:

I did not go. My sisters would not let me.

SOPHIE:

Ah! Xavier, you'll never know the talents
Of this family until you've seen
That lecture Hilda wrote, a lecture on
Astronomy. A certain star was said
To be so far away it took two men
To see it; one looked as far as possible,
The other then began where he left off.

And there's that part about the Milky Way,
So named, she said, because it was discovered
By a man who lived at Cowes, too near
The chalky cliffs of Dover.

ANTONIA:

And, Xavier,
You've yet to hear about the romance which
Elizabeth and Sophie started out
To write together.

XAVIER (*turning to Sophie and Elizabeth*):
Tell me of it. Do!

ANTONIA:

You'll not get any true account from them,
The subject is too delicate. The fact is
Sophie wrote the opening chapter and there
She introduced a heroine of such
Blue blood as made it quite impossible
To let her even glance in the direction
Of the hero that Elizabeth
Created in the second chapter, young
And handsome but, alas! a mere mechanic.
Her girl, said Sophie, could not be allowed
To marry that plebeian boy. She must,

Declared Elizabeth, or else get out
The book.

ELIZABETH:
And then—what think you?—when we turned
To our resourceful sister here to write
Our chapter three and find some way
To lift us out of our cross-purposes,
She had the hardihood to lay down this
Condition: that she be suffered to kill off,
Not one of them, but both our heroine
And hero in the selfsame accident
And start a love affair more promising.

MARIE ANNE (*rising and approaching the group*):
There's nothing so refreshes me as this
Good-natured chaff and banter, bubbling to
The surface irrepressibly whenever
You young people get together. But come.
We must not let the evening pass without
An hour of music. Marie and Xavier
I will excuse. The rest of you pray follow
To my boudoir.

(*Exeunt all except Marie Adelaide and Xavier.*) . . . .

XAVIER:

You gave me hope today. Your sisters were
Dismissed with such expressions of content-
ment
In my company. Mayhap politeness
Prompted that. But then you also spoke
Of certain qualities in me you liked.
At your dear words how much more beautiful
The whole of nature suddenly became!

There flowed in my soul, subdued and low,
Like a stream in its mossy bed,
Continuous melodies, banishing care
And bringing reflection instead.
A softer light on the beechtree played
And deeper the clover's red.

High overhead in the laughing sky
There arched a glorious bow.
The thrush and the skylark burst into song,
Singing to me, I know.
The earth was glad and the sky was glad
The moment you spoke to me so.

MARIE ADELAIDE:

All I said to you was true; liking,
Admiration, both are there. And yet

I fear I cannot reconcile myself
To thought of marriage.

XAVIER:

Your mother, sisters, and
The vast majority, I'm told, of your
Devoted subjects ardently desire
To keep you on the throne. If you will not
Agree to marry me, at least let word
Go out that we're betrothed. The Allies will
Undoubtedly consent to your remaining
On the throne with me as consort. Later
On, when you are once again secure
In your position, should you desire release
From our betrothal, I will give it you.
This plan, Marie, may not be to your liking,
But it is justified by the unreasoned
Prejudice of France which, given time,
Must surely disappear.

MARIE ADELAIDE:

How could I lend
Myself to that device? Would it not be
Deception?

No! Xavier! The Throne
I have already promised to my sister,
Charlotte. The Ministry and Parliamentary

Leaders now believe my abdication
To be necessary if Luxemburg
Is to preserve her independence. After
Giving it much thought, I have, myself,
With great reluctance, reached the same conclusion.

XAVIER:

Your decision saddens me; though I
Foresaw it. Motives governing your conduct
Are so high, unwavering and so clear
One knows beforehand on which side of any
Really serious issue you'll be found.
I made the offer in a last attempt
To have you seek to keep the dignified
Ancestral office nature fitted you
So well to fill. I knew, indeed, the chances
Were against that honest, self-denying
Soul of yours accepting it.

But if
It must be abdication, let me plead
Again the cause of your own happiness.
I love you. Come with me to Italy
As wife.

You know the rosy glow that sometimes
Fills the evening air and covers tree

And shrub. Well, just that change comes over
every
Fond relation of my life when you
Are near. I know it is the truer aspect
Of God's lovely world and 'tis the untrue
That I see when I'm away from you.
Your image is forever in my heart.
I'm conscious of it in the crowded street
And in my quiet study. At night I close
My eyes in sleep reluctant to surrender
It. At morn the distant chapel bell
Recalls that sound of silver bells—your
voice—
And brings me back to happy consciousness
Of your existence.
You will learn to love
Our Italy, will soon reflect its sunshine
In your heart.
And as for me, nor vine-clad
Hills and orange groves, nor those time-rip-
ened,
Art-filled towns will ever, in their whole
Long history, have held a happier soul;
And there have been some fervent loves be-
neath
Italian skies.

Our rustling chestnut groves
On sunny slopes are always ready to
Discourse on youth and happiness. But we
Will make the crumbling monuments and ancient
Temples talk our language, too. We'll let them
Understand that love is master in
The world; that they are there today to pleasure
Us as they did Dante and fond Petrarch
And their loves.
In springtime we will wander
In the moonlight over hills all white
With bloom of pear and cherry, stilling converse
To absorb the scene and to drink in
The flood of song from mating nightingales.

MARIE ADELAIDE:
You picture well your storied Italy
Which is already dear to me. My visit
There with Anna and with dear old Baron
Brandis, well before that tragic war
Upset the world, still lingers with me as
A lovely dream.

I'm still amused when I
Recall how Brandis grasped my skirt to keep
me
From adventuring too near the crater
Of Vesuvius. Our shoes were burned
By the hot lava flakes thrown up from out
That seething core of fire.
And ah! that sea
Of purest amethyst at fair Amalfi!
You know I was so foolish as to rush
Into it with my shoes and stockings on.

XAVIER:
Elizabeth is not the only madcap
In the family!
But, Marie,
You give me hope again. If Italy
Has found such happy lodgment in your heart,
Surrender of your childhood home will be
Less grievous. None can feel secure against
Adversity. We, too, would have our trials.
But ah! the grasp of that dear hand as wife
Would lend to me the strength of many men.
And that which most men turn to fiction for—
The romance and the poetry of life—
We'll find in all the wonder of the world
That's waiting at one's door to be invited

In. I share your lofty view, Marie,
That no man's happiness is justified
Unless it makes important contribution
To the happiness of others. It shall
Be so. For others, too, shall be the stronger,
Happier that you and I have lived.
Then, when we've travelled to the sunset hand in
Hand, we can look back with satisfaction
On the path of sun and shadow we have
Trod together.

MARIE ADELAIDE:

How few, how few the hearts
That could withstand the eloquence,
The deep sincerity and fire of your pleading!
But this poor heart of mine is set on other
Things than worldly happiness. A bride
I shall be, but a bride of Christ in holy
Church. I shall find happiness—ah, yes!
The happiness unspeakable the soul
Doth know in following the Master.

XAVIER:

Then I
Have lost my suit? Oh! do not tell me so.

MARIE ADELAIDE:

Yes, cousin. Just because there's no one, no one
I like more, I let you place the matter
Of a marriage in its happiest light
Before me. Your words were sweet to listen to.
My heart was sore and they had healing in them.
Yet now I find unaltered my deep longing
For the quiet of the cloister, for
A life of service to our Lord who suffered
All for us. I'm honored by your love,
So proud to be thus loved by such a man.
Forgive me if, in an unguarded moment,
I gave you undue hope of winning me.
You'll find a better, worthier mate to walk
Beside you through the ways of thought in which
You move so nobly. And now good-bye, my dear.
May God be with you.

XAVIER:

He will always be
With you. I pray it may not be in paths

Of suffering. Your lovely mind and person
Were not meant for that.
Believe me, I would
Give my life to spare it you.

(*Curtain*)

ACT V. SCENE I

Chamber of Deputies. Session resumed after an interval of two days.

MINISTER OF STATE:

The while that you have recessed, gentle-
men,
Our sovereign has resigned the Throne. She is
The victim of events, as conscientious
In discharge of this, her final duty
To the State (as now she sees the rendering

Up of office) as in all her public and
Her upright private life. Here is her message:
"Ever since the Government made known
To me the attitude of France toward
My person, I've been determined to lay by
The Crown. My acts are motived by a love
Of country and my desire to speed my coun-
try
On its way in moral and material
Well-being.
I hereby charge the Government
To regulate succession to the Throne,

Above all, guard my country's dearly prized
Autonomy.
The rights the smallest nations
Now enjoy, through the new charter of
The League of Nations, make it possible
For Luxemburg to shape her destiny,
God aiding her, to future peace and plenty.
My abdication takes effect at once."

(*The chamber rises and the hall is slowly emptied. A few small groups linger.*)

SCHULTZ:

The pity of it! A heart so loyal to her
Country, sensitive to every human
Call and conscious of betrayal of no
Trust to Luxemburg or to the world
Outside!

HUSS:

Aye! Aye! Humiliation wholly
Undeserved.

BECH:

Naught rankles in the breast
As does injustice. It causes men to sour
On the world, rebel against the State
And even question God's benignity.

HOFFMAN:

How true! Than that there is no greater human
Cause: in private life man's justice to his
Fellow; justice written in the law,
Administered in court, the justice practiced
By the State toward its nationals,
And justice, aye! of nation unto nation.

BRASSEUR:

The abdication was too long delayed
And it is incomplete; the dynasty
Itself should go.

AUGUST THORN:

By no means. Crushing out
Despotic rule like that of Germany
And Russia, I admit, was justified.
In Russia, which had known the knout, corruption
Was proverbial and the masses groaned
Beneath a reign of terror. Ruthless, brutal
Bolshevism there is but th' explosion
Of the people's wrath, the bursting of
Their chains. And that upheaval, prompted for
Strategic reasons by imperialists

In Germany, by a queer turn of fate,
Invaded Germany itself, as well as
Austria-Hungary, that Germany
Where one man had had everything to say
And where a word from him let loose a war
Which sowed the seeds of ruin everywhere
And cost the lives of millions.
But, my dear sir,
No such conditions have existed here.
We men of Luxemburg are free, as free
As people anywhere. What call have we
To overthrow our dynasty? The need is
To suppress forthwith the lawlessness
That marks the present agitation. Those
Who started it are largely unknown men;
They are not authorized to speak for us.

HUSS:
The grave injustice of this morning's doings
Must have caused our Duchess' heart to bleed.
And yet no outward sign of it! Was not
Her message goddess-like, with all the sorrow
Of the world in that great heart unspoken?

BECH:
No, no! Complaint she may not utter: her nature

Is too deep for that. But she must ever
Hold us an ungrateful lot, for we have
Brought her disillusionment profound
And filled her future days with pain. A whole
life
Led in lowly walks holds no such wormwood
As does greatness lost.

HOFFMAN:

Nor is she of
The kind who plunge in pleasure's stream to
drink
The waters of forgetfulness.

(*Curtain*)

ACT V. SCENE II

Scene: Marie Adelaide's Boudoir. Her mother, five sisters and Anna Montgelas are seen seated.

MARIE ANNE:

How silent and how sad our dinner was!
Our Marie was the only one of us
Who kept her spirits up. To my surprise,
Her sparkling eyes and happy face betokened
Looked-for pleasure. I could not blame you for

Your failure to respond. Myself, I found it
Quite impossible to lay aside
The thought of parting with her, the thought
That this was her last dinner in her home.

CHARLOTTE:

And when she rose and bade us follow her,
Her eyes were livelier than ever. Clearly
Something of importance is afoot.
All day she's kept herself aloof. Her maid
Alone had access to her, busied, I am
Told, with packing and unpacking boxes.
'Tis some surprise she has in store for us
Else there would not have been this secrecy.
But here our darling sister comes.

(*Marie Adelaide enters from her bedroom, followed by two maids laden with caskets, furs and gowns. They open the caskets and place them on a table. The furs and gowns they place on chairs and then leave the room.*)

MARIE ADELAIDE:

You,
My Mother, must choose first.

(*Marie Anne, choking with emotion, moves over to the table and takes the nearest casket without a glance at its contents.*)

And you, my sisters,
Will not mind if I divide the rest
In equal parts, including a full share
For Countess Anna, whom, you know, I often
Term "Sixth Sister." She has meant so much
To me.
To Lotta, our new sovereign,
Must go this rope of pearls and coronet
I wore when I was crowned six years and eight
Short months ago. This emerald Sophie often
Has admired and it shall be among
The things I give to her. This bracelet Hilda
Likes, that diamond brooch Elizabeth.
And here's a collar, pearls and diamonds,
For our Antonia. It will be nice
To think of each of you as wearing these,
The jewels that you favored. The rings and furs
And all the other articles I leave you
To partition as you will.

MARIE ANNE:

'Tis plain,
A plea to have you change your mind
About them would be vain, Marie; but you
Must realize this distribution of

Your cherished things gives all of us more pain
Than pleasure.

CHARLOTTE:

You ought not to sever all
The ties that bind you to a lovely, useful
Past.

HILDA:

Do keep the things, Marie, oh do!

MARIE ADELAIDE:

I understand. But of what earthly use
Could sparkling jewels, furs and gowns like
these
Now be to me? No! No! You must accept
them
And can do so with an easy conscience.
Our parting is the cruel thing. Each
Of you so dear to me! The fond familiar
Scenes I leave behind! But I embrace
With actual joy the richer life I am
About to enter.

I want to read to you
My farewell message to my people. It
Reveals my real feelings, now the struggle

With myself is over: glad acceptance
Of what He decrees.
When doubt beset me,
Finally there came, in answer to my
Prayers, this quieting resolve: "Whatever
You can do in line of duty do it
Cheerfully and what you cannot do
Don't worry over." In face of France's plain
Hostility, I saw I could no longer
Stay upon the Throne. With that conviction,
Prospect of a life in holy walks
Came as the vision of a land of promise,
Filled me, yes! with joy.
I liked my office
As the head of this, our snug and compact
Land. However little I myself
Contributed in thought or action to
The public weal, the consciousness of service
Still was there. The measures daily laid
Before me made me feel that I was not
An unimportant part of the machinery
Of State. And who, that trusts himself, dis-
likes
Authority?
But, 'mid the practical,
The soul is oft athirst for higher things,

The spirit's longings go unsatisfied.
That need is real and one suffers if
It is denied. To this neglected need
I now can give attention, following paths
In which the soul may grow.
Now, hear the message;
I need to know it meets with your approval.

MONTGELAS:
Marie appeared last night at midnight in
My room with pad and pencil, told me what
She had in mind and sat there shivering
By my bed in her thin robe, despite
My protest, framing this courageous message.
Ah! we know, Marie, it wrung your heart
To write it. She wrote it straight away without
Corrections.

MARIE ADELAIDE:
I'd thought it out, lying awake
In bed, before I went to Anna's room.
Words are but the garments placed on thought.
The taste I show in their selection may not
Be the best, but I have never found it
Difficult to put the garments on.
(Reads)
"From every part of Luxemburg have come

Such tokens of devotion. My thanks and deepest
Gratitude to you, my people, for them.
My heart is filled with happiness. That love
Of country, which has ever been my guide,
Makes easy this last sacrifice. My thought,
My prayers will ever be for my beloved
Home.
Its destinies have now been placed
In worthy hands. I ask that to my sister,
Your new ruler, you display the same
Fidelity, the same self-sacrifice
You showed and practiced toward me. Continue
To be true, free Luxemburgers, faithful
Children of our Holy Church. May God
And Blessed Virgin, refuge of afflicted
Souls, ever point the way."

MARIE ANNE:

The message
Is indeed courageous. What is more,
As uttered in my Marie's lovely voice,
It seemed a benediction.

ANTONIA:

Her voice itself
Is that.

(*Curtain*)

ACT V. SCENE III

(*A lapse of five years*)

Scene: Castle of Hohenburg. Marie Adelaide on her deathbed, Marie Anne seated beside her, weeping silently.

MARIE ADELAIDE:

I know that I shall soon be leaving you;
My strength is waning hourly. The fever
That impaired it while in Italy
Has laid its deadly hold on me again
And this time means to conquer.

MARIE ANNE:

No! No! You must not
Cease to hope and will to live. Oft when
The flame of life is flickering, the issue
Hangs on that. You know how dear you are
To us; we want you so. You're young, and years
Of happiness should still be yours.

MARIE ADELAIDE (*pausing frequently to regain strength enough to go on*):

My childhood
And my early womanhood were happy,

Oh! so happy! Ah! those wondrous days
Amid the roses of our Luxemburg!
The hours that sped on wingèd feet among
The pine clad hills of the Bavarian Alps!
Your own and Anna's care of me! (*Pause*)
Do you
Recall the day I wandered far afield,
Was late in getting back and how you came
To meet me, far, so very far from home?

MARIE ANNE:
As if 'twere yesterday. You were expected
Back at noon, and when the sun had set
With nothing seen of you, ashamed to let
My fears be known, I went alone to seek you.

MARIE ADELAIDE:
How fathomless the sky that Autumn day!
What sparkle in the air! I drank it deep
And climbed and climbed with ease to such a
height
The cattle in the vale below seemed mice.
(*Pause*)
I recollect—I must have told you at
The time—how I had settled in a warm
And sunny spot to write some childish verses,

How I fell asleep on a deep bed
Of sweet pine needles blown against a rock.
(*Pause*)
Then when I saw my Mother, looking for
Her missing child on that steep mountainside,
I knew what place I must have in your heart.
(*Pause*)
An unseen hand had drawn aside a curtain
And there stood revealed to me the power
And the magic of that wondrous thing,
A mother's love. (*Pause*)
Your wilful, thoughtless child
Came later on to know it as the purest,
Most unselfish and self-sacrificing,
Yes! the noblest force in that wide range
Of motive that so sways the living world.
(*Pause*)
From full awakening to that truth I date
My aim, imperfect, feeble though it was,
To lay aside my own blind selfishness
And follow where I thought my duty led.
(*Pause*)
Then, too, the dear companionship of sisters
With their merry ways!

Who ever had
Such sunny childhood and such golden youth
As mine?

MARIE ANNE:

And with what suddenness, alas!
Poor child, all this was changed!

MARIE ADELAIDE:

And I remember
Too, how when I was about to start
On my official visits to the German,
Dutch and Belgian Courts and asked you what
Advice you had to give to me, you showed
Your confidence in me by answering simply
"Smile, my child."

MARIE ANNE:

It was the sole instruction
Needed. No one could, I knew, resist
That lovely smile of yours.

MARIE ADELAIDE:

My cares began
With the responsibilities of rule,
And, when that frightful war burst on th' astonished
World, they multiplied. (*Pause*)

To your advice
I owe that pleasant year in Switzerland
Before I settled down in Italy.
A searching of the soul there was, the need
To fix the where and when of convent life.
But it was lightened for me by the friends
Who sought me out. (*Pause*)
Perhaps the happiest hours
Were those I spent with Anna at Spiez.
We swept its little chapel, dusted benches,
Washed and mended chapel linen, kept
Its altar bright with alpen-rosen, gentian,
Mountain lilies. Oh! we found such joy
In wandering o'er the countryside in search
Of them.

MARIE ANNE:

You always loved the open. Is it
Not because one's thoughts are healthier,
Saner there?

MARIE ADELAIDE:

Perhaps! I had not thought of it
That way. (*Pause*)
There lingers in my mind that motor
Trip by night with Karl to witness Lotta's

Wedding to his consort's brother. A proxy
Marriage is a cold affair.

MARIE ANNE:

A play
With an important character left out.
And poor, dear Karl! The head of such an ancient
House as that of Hapsburg stepping down
From that proud throne! There could have been but little
Gaiety in such a group.

MARIE ADELAIDE:

And yet
To me the ceremony brought the deepest
Satisfaction: it meant a direct heir
To our Throne, a matter both of us
Have had so much at heart.

The rigors of
The life in Italy I did not mind.
I chose it of my own free will.

MARIE ANNE:

Alas!
'Twas overmuch for you, my child.

MARIE ADELAIDE:

But such
Contentment came of hourly worship in
The Convent Chapel and the quiet cell,
And, later, of the work among the poor.
While serving their great need I seemed to see
The Master walking by my side, as prescient
Xavier in substance once foretold. (*Pause*)
My lengthy vigils in the convent cell
Brought out more clearly to me one great truth
But dimly realized before. 'Tis this:
There is a knowable world which God permits us
To behold and, yes! increasingly
To understand. And close beside it lies
Another world our understanding is
Unequal to and ever will be. We cannot
Think of space as something without limit.
And if we try to picture it as having
Limit, we ask ourselves at once what is
Beyond that outer boundary of space.
To answer "nothing" helps us not at all;
For "nothing" is but empty space to us. (*Pause*)
The same is true of time. We cannot think of
It as having always been, nor are

Our minds so framed that we can say "Once
time
Was not." And so I let my faith reach far
Beyond my understanding. That way wisdom
Lies and strength to serve and to endure.
(*Long pause*)
Though short, my life has been a wondrous one.
And now that He, The Master, says "enough,"
I go, my Mother, with a smile.
All things that had beginning, must have end.
'Tis God
Alone's without beginning, without end.
(*Pause*)
I would have loved to see my Luxemburg
Once more, its people and its hills. I was
So happy there. My people, too, loved me.
I know, I know they loved me, and will hold
My memory dear. The enemies I had
Were few. They triumphed but because of
foreign
Pressure, pressure which our little land
Could not withstand.
I'm tired, so tired! Your wish
Has been my law. Now tell me I
May go. And let me hold your hand as I

Drop off asleep. That hand still links me close
To all that's dear to me.

(*She closes her eyes. The family and attendants are summoned; and, while they converse in anxious, subdued tones, Marie Adelaide passes away in her sleep.*)

MARIE ANNE:

Dear God! She's gone.
My darling, darling child! (*All kneel.*)

(*Curtain*)